At the
CROSSROADS

Other Abingdon Press Books from Clayton Smith

Propel: Good Stewardship, Greater Generosity

AT THE
CROSSROADS

Leadership Lessons for the Second Half of Life

Clayton Smith & Dave Wilson

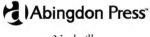

Abingdon Press™

Nashville

AT THE CROSSROADS:
LEADERSHIP LESSONS FOR THE SECOND HALF OF LIFE

This book is printed on acid-free paper.

ISBN: 978-1-5018-1050-3

Unless otherwise indicated, all scripture quotations are from the Common English Bible. Copyright © 2011 by the Common English Bible. All rights reserved. Used by permission. www.CommonEnglishBible.com.

Scripture quotations marked MSG are from THE MESSAGE. Copyright © by Eugene H. Peterson 1993, 1994, 1995, 1996, 2000, 2001, 2002. Used by permission of NavPress Publishing Group.

16 17 18 19 20 21 22 23 24 25—10 9 8 7 6 5 4 3 2 1
MANUFACTURED IN THE UNITED STATES OF AMERICA

CONTENTS

Visit Cokesbury.com to download a free leader's guide PDF. Password on page 90.

INTRODUCTION

In recent years, we have been hearing our church members ask, "What do I need to do to be ready for retirement? I want the next part of my life to be the best. I want to make a significant difference!"

Since January 1, 2014, as many as 10,000 men and women turn sixty-five each day in the United States. By 2030, when the last of the baby boomer generation turns sixty-five (these are the people who turned fifty in 2014), 18 percent of the population will be sixty-five and older. But don't talk to this generation about old age or retirement.[1]

Most people who approach or turn sixty-five don't think of themselves as "old" and many dislike or are anxious about the idea of retirement. They wonder what they will do and want a life in retirement that is meaningful and significant. Yet retirement without adequate thought can become frustrating, confusing, and stressful.

In the last ten years in our local church, we have seen the age-fifty-and-over membership grow by more than 500 percent! Have you seen similar growth of baby boomers in your church and community? How is the church going to reach this fifties-and-over age group?

For many, there may be a lack of purpose, significance, and identity. We have seen many people who are at the prime of their life miss out on opportunities that bring fulfillment and joy. We hear too many stories about friends and neighbors who fall into a retirement syndrome that may lead to distress, anxiety, depression, divorce, poor health, or even suicide. Many worry about the increased costs of health care and financial resources necessary to sustain a longer life. How can the church respond to this age group? This Bible-based, six-week small group study offers hope and help! This study is about living a healthy second half of life with purpose. Purpose has a powerful way of bringing health and happiness into our lives and the lives of people around us. God gives us purpose.

By following biblical principles from the lives of Moses, Abraham, Elijah, Nehemiah, Jesus, and Paul, as well as other encouraging Bible passages, you can realize your purpose, passion, and mission for the second half of life.

This study is not about planning a retirement that is fiscally secure and physically healthy. This study is about developing a spiritually significant approach to retirement that will add joy to your life, years to your life, and life to your years! We want to help you choose the road to significance through spiritual lessons to guide the second half of your life!

Discovering your life story is one way of finding God's plan for you. As you will seek answers about God's calling on your life and see how you can contribute significantly to the lives of others, you will understand how your life lessons, skills, and experiences can be used to better serve others. You will find greater fulfillment in doing so.

This workbook includes planning tools to develop unique personal and spiritual mission statements to enrich the lives of those who are anticipating retirement in the near future or years from now, as well as the lives of those who have already retired. The study also features interviews and stories from those who have faced the challenges and have successfully transitioned into new lives with significance. Be sure to check out the online Leader's Guide for more in-depth teaching aids for your small group or class at Cokesbury.com.

To prepare for each class, read the scripture passages and answer questions in the Understanding the Bible Story section. Take notes so you can fully participate in class discussion. Write down answers to key questions. The scripture discussion in class can help you clarify and execute the next steps in the study.

As you complete the Experiencing Your Life Story section during the week, you will map out your journey into retirement. Through a self-inventory, you can discover your spiritual gifts, talents, resources, individuality, desires, experience, and seasons of life. This inventory can also provide information about areas of service that fit your unique needs for serving others. Be prepared to discuss your story in a class or your small group as a way to encourage one another.

At the end of each chapter are tools to help you work through the study and information on additional sources of materials to enhance your study and planning for the second half of your life.

The best is yet to be!

Discovering Your Life Story

Scripture Verse

Stop at the crossroads and look around; / ask for the ancient paths. / Where is the good way? / Then walk in it / and find a resting place for yourselves.

—Jeremiah 6:16

> *All we have to do [for retirement] is to listen to ourselves, embrace our enthusiasm, and get involved.*
>
> *—Roger Staubach*

Opening Prayer

Dear God of the Ages, give us wisdom as we search for the right route to follow into the second half of our lives. Lead us to the good way. In Jesus's name. Amen.

Introduction

The second half of life is about the significant difference you can make for others.

It is about your creative opportunities to change lives.

It is about your impact on family, friends, church, and community.

It is about the joy of leaving a legacy for those you love.

3

It is about the benefit of a group study where you can learn from each other.
It is about discovering new fun, fellowship, and faith experiences!

Getting to Know You

Tell us about yourself (name, hometown, family, career, and how long you've been attending church).

Will You Have a Purpose-filled Second Half of Life?

In this chapter, you will begin to answer this question. You can learn how to claim your life story, consider the biblical story, and make choices to help you live a full life of significance.

Each chapter in this study will give you guidance and insight to develop your own purpose-filled retirement plan that will bring a healthy lifestyle for your body, mind, and spirit. This study captures the stories of a number of members of The United Methodist Church of the Resurrection in the Kansas City area. The church's own story is really about a growing number of members of all ages who have discovered a faith-based purpose and are making significant differences in changing lives, influencing the community and world, and bringing renewal to the church.

> *Purpose has a powerful way of bringing health and happiness into our lives and the lives of those around us.*

Researchers are studying ways to encourage better mental vitality in older adults. Dr. Patricia Boyle, a neuropsychologist and researcher, claims that the research has discovered a way to slow cognitive decline in adults by 30 percent. Those who reported that they lived with a purpose showed a slower rate of cognitive decline than those who did not. Having a purpose and plan for your retirement life can reduce the risk of dementia problems, such as Alzheimer's.[1] People who live purposeful lives are those who have significant goals. By discovering and working toward your goals in retirement, you enhance your brain's memory and capacity. Pursuing your purpose is vitally important to the rest of your life.

> *Instead, we are God's accomplishment, created in Christ Jesus to do good things. God planned for these good things to be the way that we live our lives.*
>
> —*Ephesians 2:10*

God gives you a purpose. Once you discover and pursue your purpose, you find greater joy.

Dave's Story

The little gods in our lives are supposedly inoffensive; there is really not anything wrong with them, but they can grow into idols that consume our time and resources and keep us from doing something significant in God's eyes.

What are the little gods in my life? I love my family and grandchildren; I have always had a passion for golf and for the University of Kansas basketball. As I entered retirement, I had to decide how I would spend my time in following these passions and other interests without them becoming idols. I had to consider how my faith and my commitment to God would affect my new life.

Before retirement, I served as Congregational Care Minister, small group leader, and in other areas of the church that needed specific help. These involved other people in so many ways that the blessings flowed constantly to others as well as to me. But if I decided that I could play golf almost every day and spend time with my buddies in the clubhouse, how much energy and time would I have to spend on faith-related activities and family? I had to take seriously that the scriptures were telling me to devote my life to God—not golf—and that in doing so I would choose life and blessings.

What blessings or curses might my choices produce for me? If I choose too much leisure, I could lose focus on people; if I do not keep up my exercise, I lose my health.

If I choose to serve, I might gain many new relationships with people at church and see how walking alongside or teaching made a difference to someone else. Putting aside time for more family activity could mean so many more memories, love, and favor without the regrets that so often come during a career.

In my "before" life, I was accountable to my boss; in my family, to my wife, my mother, children, and extended members; and in church, to God. I am still accountable to my family members and to God, but now that I no longer have a boss overseeing my daily work, I realize that I must schedule my time even better than I did during my career. Deciding how to spend each day requires discipline. It's all too easy to procrastinate. I needed someone to talk to about my comings and goings. I found an accountability partner, a church friend who was interested in weekly conversations over coffee or on the phone, or by text at almost any time. This has helped me find balance in leisure, exercise, relationships, service, and in my time with and for God.

Whom will I serve this day? I can only say that I have to choose God and life, and it starts each day.

Questions for Discussion

1. What are the key elements to Dave's story?

2. Where are you in the transition process?

3. What might be the next steps you take toward exploring all the possibilities for the second half of life?

Understanding the Bible Story

Joshua says, "But if it seems wrong in your opinion to serve the LORD, then choose today whom you will serve. Choose the gods whom your ancestors served beyond the Euphrates or the gods of the Amorites in whose land you live. But my family and I will serve the LORD" (Josh 24:15).

Moses says, "I call heaven and earth as my witnesses against you right now: I have set life and death, blessing and curse before you. Now choose life—so that your descendants will live" (Deut 30:19).

Elijah proclaims, "'How long will you hobble back and forth between two opinions? If the LORD is God, follow God. If Baal is God, follow Baal.' The people gave no answer" (1 Kgs 18:21).

Read Deuteronomy 30. Moses and the Israelites are looking across the Jordan River into the promised land. They have wandered around in the wilderness for forty years and now are ready to take possession of the lands that God had promised their ancestors hundreds of years earlier.

What does Moses say will happen?

_____

_____

_____

What does God promise to do?

_____

_____

_____

What did Moses say you must do in order to claim these promises as yours?

_____

_____

_____

Small Group Discussion Questions

What are the current little gods or idols that people worship?

_____

_____

_____

What choices do you face?

_____

_____

_____

Which of these choices might be worshipping little gods?

_____

_____

_____

How might your choice affect others who are close to you or perhaps people you do not even know?

_____

_____

_____

Moses called heaven and earth as witnesses as he challenged the people. Who might be a witness to whom you can be accountable?

_____

_____

_____

Moses says that he has set before the people life and death, blessings and curses that you will experience because of your choice of whom to serve. What might be some blessings or curses that you might receive depending on your future choices?

_____

_____

_____

How does God show you mercy, favor, and love?

_____

_____

_____

Your career may have been successful in many ways. But what opportunities do you think you might have lost, delayed, or missed while you worked?

_____

_____

_____

Whatever they are, God offers an opportunity to reclaim your heart's desires. You can choose the road into the promise land of retirement with greater faith and focus on life abundant. Start your journey now!

Is there any reason not to serve the Lord? If not, when will you start?

_____

_____

_____

Experiencing Your Life Story

All of the events concerning Moses, Joshua, and Elijah were transition points in their lives and the lives of their families and community. The Israelites were ready to enter the promised land, a land filled with wonderful new opportunities, especially after living in the desert for forty years. Moses's challenge is to lead the people and prepare them to enter the promised land. Joshua's challenge occurs after the Israelites had conquered the promised land. Elijah's challenge happens when the people follow foreign gods, which in this case had much to do with personal pleasures.

> *They are like a tree replanted by streams of water,*
> *which bears fruit at just the right time.*
>
> *—Psalm 1:3a*

Paul writes to the Ephesians that in Christ the Father "poured over us" God's overflowing grace (Eph 1:8). When God outdoes God's self for your good, life becomes greater than you could ask for or imagine (cf. Eph 3:20). This means that your life after retirement can be filled with blessed times. As you approach retirement or if you have already entered it, new opportunities lay ahead, opportunities to lay up treasures in heaven. You can come to know God better, love God more deeply, and serve God more effectively (see Tool A: Examples of Opportunities to Be Involved).

You no longer have bosses or supervisors to tell you what time to show up for work, what time to leave, or how to fill your day. You simply need to do what needs to be done. How will you claim God's promises declared by Moses in Deuteronomy 30? What you chose will bring you blessings or curses, even life or death. Chose life—a life of significance!

EXAMPLES OF OPPORTUNITIES TO BE INVOLVED

Sample Opportunities

Here is an example of the type of information that might be helpful for people who want to become involved in growing their Christian faith, improving their community, and strengthening the church. This example is from our church, The United Methodist Church of the Resurrection.

- Adults are invited to join the journey of a lifetime, the journey of knowing, loving, and serving God through study. Adult studies include the Alpha class, Journey 101, Bible studies, Disciple Bible Study, and Group Life as well as seminary-style classes with the top professors from a local seminary.

- Ministries are divided into singles, women, men, college life, twenty-somethings, boomers, seniors, and neighborhoods.

- Service or mission opportunities are available to serve at church, in Kansas City, and beyond Kansas City. Local programs include Backpacks for Hunger that provides packages of food to elementary students to take home over the weekend; partnering with urban schools to provide minor repairs, painting, playgrounds, tutoring, mentoring, and books; and FaithWorks twice monthly on Saturdays to serve others in church and community. In addition, J.O.Y. in Service provides food and gifts that are collected and distributed during winter holidays.

- The Missions Team oversees the Bed Ministry, Furnishings Ministry, Cars Ministry, Clothing Ministries, Food Ministry, Hunger Ministry, Computer Ministry, and Housing Ministry.

- In Justice and Reconciliation, programs serve A Child's Hope foster parenting, Veronica's Voice, Healing House, and Prison Ministry.

- In economic development are the Co-Op and Urban Development teams.

- Disaster response teams help at both small and large events. Community blood drives and the Golf Classic also need many volunteers.

- Music and worship offer opportunities in choirs and bands for all ages and talents. The need for greeters, ushers, and people behind the scenes is vast.

- Student Ministries need volunteers at Youth Group, Sunday school, confirmation classes, Group Life leaders, and mission trips. Youth mission trips are scheduled each year.

- The Children's Ministry (Kids COR) has opportunities every day of the week.

- Matthew's Ministry provides Sunday school, mission, and recreation opportunities for children and adults with developmental disabilities.

- Congregational Care Ministry (CCM) teams of lay members support the pastoral staff in caring for members of the congregation who are ill, going through difficult times, experiencing life changes, or just need someone to walk alongside them.

- Care Night provides fellowship, spiritual encouragement, and support groups. These classes are ongoing as well as one-time seminars.

- The Recreation Ministry sponsors events in tennis, golf, softball, volleyball, kickball, car shows, basketball, dodgeball, and bridge. There is also Rez Riders (motorcycles) and the Painters Art Guild.

- Crossroads Ministry for those over fifty offers classes, small groups, preretirement seminars, social events, Medicare and Social Security workshops, and estate planning events.

TRANSITIONS: CHANGES, CHALLENGES, AND OPPORTUNITIES

Scripture Verse

Instead, we are God's accomplishment, created in Christ Jesus to do good things. God planned for these good things to be the way that we live our lives.

—Ephesians 2:10

Opening Prayer

Dear Lord God, you are the same yesterday, today, and tomorrow. You do not change. But our human lives are full of change. Lead us as we look for your purpose to guide our lives. In the name of Jesus. Amen.

> *Don't let me live to be useless.*
>
> *—John Wesley, founder of Methodism*

Introduction

Our world is going through a major transition. The number of older adults worldwide will increase at an alarming rate during the next three decades. Is this for the better or worse? One perspective is positive. This view argues that older adults are inspiring role models. Members of the baby boomer generation (1946–1965) have proven survival skills and are becoming pioneers on aging well while living much longer.

The other perspective is less encouraging. This view argues that this tsunami of older people will put an increased burden on our social, health care, and financial resources.

Getting to Know You

Do you see this demographic transition as an opportunity or burden? Which stage of the transition are you in?

- Preretirement
- Early retirement
- Mid-retirement
- Late retirement

Will You Have a Purpose-Filled Second Half of Life?

In this chapter, you will have an opportunity to ask yourself, "What do I need to do to find purpose in the rest of my life?" Below are ten questions to ponder. In chapters 3 and 4, you will have a chance to dig deeper into these questions. Right now, just consider:

How can you grow a vibrant relationship with God?

_____

_____

_____

What do you want to do to experience joy?

_____

_____

_____

How can you carry out your lifelong learning quest?

_____

_____

_____

How can you model Christian character in the way you live?

_____

_____

_____

What do you need to do to be committed to loving, knowing, and serving Christ?

_____

_____

_____

How can you best witness the joy of generosity?

_____

_____

_____

Have you planned a lasting legacy?

_____

_____

_____

How will your witness change lives for Christ?

_____

_____

_____

How do you best do mission outreach to those in need?

_____

_____

_____

As you face the changes, challenges, and opportunities in the transition into retirement, contemplate: *"What will I do with the rest of my life?"*

Mark and Kim's Story

(As told by Pastor Clayton Smith)

When I first met Mark and Kim at a Crown Financial Bible Study, they were preparing for Mark's retirement as a federal bank examiner. Kim was a part-time interior decorator, homemaker, and mother of their two children. Even though they were in their fifties, they wanted to set up a faith-based budget for their retirement years. Mark and Kim stood out as exceptional leaders and were committed to serving in our church.

When I asked Mark and Kim about how their careers had prepared them for retirement, I discovered that Mark's work with the Office of the Comptroller of the Currency offered a helpful preretirement seminar. Mark's career was all about financial best practices. But their Christian faith was informed by the Bible. Mark and Kim were going to live the second half of their lives in service to others.

They both loved meeting people. They had lived in four or five different communities when work required transfers. Each move prepared them to meet new people and situations with delight and satisfaction. They became involved in their neighborhood, church, and their children's activities. Connection was the key for them!

Their view of retirement was summed up in two words: flexibility and excitement. While Kim's homemaker role did not change much, she was eager to learn about opportunities to partner with Mark in service to our church. I invited Mark and Kim to become class coordinators for our new Financial Peace University (FPU) course. They are a great team! They have now coordinated nineteen courses, teaching more than seven hundred students.

With great eagerness, Mark helped launch a new financial coaching ministry. Again, his professional experience as a federal bank examiner prepared him to help us help others. The program quickly grew. It now includes many coaches to serve people who seek to set up personal budgets and eliminate debt.

Mark and Kim found the FPU budgeting principles to be most helpful in establishing their own personal retirement spending plan. Since it worked well for them, they knew it could help others in their classes. They lead by example! In their retirement, their leadership in our financial ministry will continue for years to come. They have the spiritual gifts of teaching, encouragement, and leadership, and a passion for helping those who need hope and practical help. I have seen them become "lifesavers" to others who struggled with finances, which often causes conflict in marriage.

Their purpose statement for life is found in their priorities. They believe in putting God first, family second, others third, and occupation last. Mark reports that he thinks about this set of priorities almost every day. When he was working in his career, his job was a priority, but it was last on the list. Kim reported that this priority list reduced Mark's anxiety and brought greater joy to his life. And now, they both find joy every day, especially in serving others.

God has prepared and blessed Mark and Kim in the second half of their lives. They are committed to keeping busy. They are energized. There is no time for taking naps. They want to have fun, to witness their faith, and to use their freedom to change lives. They continuously think of new ways to help others.

Their adult Sunday school class is filled with people like Mark and Kim who are serving God with their heads, hearts, and hands to transform our community. What they are doing is multiplied by their examples of leadership. Of course, they would humbly say, "There are so many better examples of leadership in our church." I would gratefully say, "Thank God for all of our leaders who, like Mark and Kim, are taking the changes and challenges of their retirement years and transforming them into opportunities to serve with joy!"

Questions for Discussion

1. What are the key elements of this story?

_____

_____

_____

2. In what ways do you identify with the story?

_____

_____

_____

3. What are your next steps?

_____

_____

_____

Understanding the Bible Story

Read Exodus 3:1-12 about Moses at the burning bush. Moses is eighty years old. He is doing his day job and encounters a strange sight, a bush that is burning, but is not consumed. The bush also speaks to him. This is how God appeared to Moses.

> *Moses said to God, "Who am I to go to Pharaoh and to bring the Israelites out of Egypt?"*
>
> *—Exodus 3:11*

How did Moses react when he saw this strange sight and heard God's voice?

_____

_____

_____

What did Moses learn about God?

_____

_____

_____

Why was Moses afraid?

_____

_____

_____

When you met God for the first time, what was your reaction? What did you expect? (If you have not met God as Jesus Christ, please see your leader after class for more information.)

_____

_____

_____

Read Exodus 3:13-22. Moses asks for God's name.

What did Moses learn next about God, who God was, and how Moses was to carry out God's plan?

_____

_____

_____

> *God said to Moses, "I Am Who I Am. So say to the Israelites, 'I Am has sent me to you.'"*
>
> —*Exodus 3:14*

What did Moses learn about his own heart?

_____

_____

_____

What did you learn about how God operates?

_____

_____

_____

Read Genesis 12:1-9. Abram was seventy-five years old, living with his family in Ur of the Chaldeans, which is in modern-day Iraq. Ur was a prosperous city and had many conveniences for its time. God called Abram to leave his familiar surroundings, extended family, and friends and to go to a place he had never been before.

> *The LORD said to Abram, "Leave your land, your family, and your father's household for the land that I will show you."*
>
> —*Genesis 12:1*

Where do you see the first evidence of Abram's belief in God?

_____

_____

_____

What differences in behavior did you see between verses 7 and 8? Why is this important?

_____

_____

_____

What did you learn in the passage that is significant to you?

_____

_____

_____

Small Group Discussion Questions

When people first meet God, many usually have the same reactions and expectations as Moses. Facing a holy God may scare people because of what they have done or not done. Like Moses, they come to realize they are not worthy of standing on holy ground. They may expect judgment or punishment. They may not know much about God or God's grace and what God wants them to do with the knowledge of who God is.

What do you know about God? (Personal)

_____

_____

_____

How do you see yourself in your retirement years? Will you be a contributor or a liability to others?

_____

_____

_____

How can you promote the well-being and affirm the dignity of others?

_____

_____

_____

How can you be a positive role model and encourage others who are moving or have moved into retirement?

_____

_____

_____

Experiencing Your Life Story

Regardless of your retirement stage, you can discover and experience more of life. As you clarify your purpose, each day you can wake excited to get up and get going. As you approach retirement, you will be asked often what you plan to do. Many people think retirement is about playing golf, taking long vacations, sitting at home watching television, puttering around in the yard, lounging around the pool, or indulging in rest and relaxation. Yes, those might be fun for a while. But after about two weeks, most people want to do something else. Something with purpose.

Retirement means you have a greater say in what you do and when you do it. Regardless of your retirement stage—whether preretirement or retired for a long time—you can choose activities that will make a positive difference in your life and in the lives of others. The most important quest is to find significant purpose in each day. Retirement offers time and opportunities to

- Be with family and close friends, nurturing and cherishing those relationships.
- Mentor and coach others.
- Reach out to people who are hungry, thirsty, naked, and sick, and to those in prison (Matt 25:37-40).
- Witness your faith by practicing the "apostolic model" of discipleship.
- Make a friend.
- Be a friend.
- Lead a friend to Christ.

As you refine your purpose in retirement, seek wisdom from the Lord about when to say no to opportunities that do not fit your mission statement (which we'll discuss in chapter 4), and when to say yes—even when you are not sure you can handle what the Lord is calling you to do. Like Abram, look for a way of life that will bless you to be a blessing. Answer the following questions:

- What are you already qualified to do?
- What hobbies do you have?
- How can you balance the use of your time, resources, and money?
- Who might help you evaluate your potential ministry skills?
- Do you have any physical limitations?
- What training would you need?

Troubled times and uncertainty emphasize the need to recognize the importance of a spiritually significant retirement plan. Without such a plan, life may be sweet and easy, but it may also be short and less significant than we want it to be. You now have two lifetimes. One is as you grow up, mature, and start jobs and families. The other consists of the life after all that. How will you spend your second lifetime?

⊷ Tool B ⊶
SPIRITUAL GIFTS INVENTORY

> *We have different gifts that are consistent with God's grace that has been given to us. If your gift is prophecy, you should prophesy in proportion to your faith. If your gift is service, devote yourself to serving. If your gift is teaching, devote yourself to teaching. If your gift is encouragement, devote yourself to encouraging. The one giving should do it with no strings attached. The leader should lead with passion. The one showing mercy should be cheerful.*
>
> *—Romans 12:6-8*

You have your own spiritual gifts, granted by the Lord to achieve the Lord's purpose for you. There are at least thirty spiritual gifts found in scripture. The following are some of the spiritual gifts that can make a difference in how you serve your church and community. Put a check mark by your spiritual gifts.

_____ Speaking the truth, prophecy

_____ Serving, helping, being in mission

_____ Teaching, researching, and speaking

_____ Encouraging and caring

_____ Giving and managing resources

_____ Leading others and executing plans

_____ Offering mercy, compassion, and comfort

_____ Having wisdom and insight, and advising

_____ Having knowledge, studying, and discovering

_____ Offering hospitality and welcome

If you have not taken a spiritual gifts inventory, you can do so now at http://www.umc.org/what-we-believe/spiritual-gifts-online-assessment. If you have not taken the inventory in recent years, take it again. Many people at retirement stages of life find that their spiritual gifts have changed through maturity. Spiritual gifts classes may be available through your church or online. Retirement is a great time to really serve God! Deploy your gifts in service to others and find joy!

We recommend a very helpful resource: *Serving from the Heart: Finding Your Gifts and Talents for Serving.*[1]

Chapter 3
SEEKING A HIGHER PURPOSE

Scripture Verse

Your hands fashioned and made me.

—Job 10:8a

Opening Prayer

Dear God who provides, you have a plan and a purpose for me that does not end with retirement. Thank you for all the experiences, talents, and skills you have given me so far. Help me use them to honor you in all I do. In Jesus's name. Amen.

> *I am what I am by God's grace.*
>
> *—1 Corinthians 15:10*

Introduction

Life teaches that each one of us is unique. God has shaped every person and has planned for that person to fulfill a purpose and to be significant. Are you seeking a higher purpose, especially for the second half of your life?

Getting to Know You

What do you do for fun?

Will You Have a Purpose-Filled Second Half of Life?

When you reach the preretirement or early retirement phases, you may begin to ask what you can do to make a difference. You may ask questions like the following:

- I believe there is something more in life that God wants me to do. How do I discover it?

- How can I feel more fulfilled and fruitful in the church?

- Is there something wrong with me because I don't know how to enjoy retirement?

- Why am I asked to do the things I don't enjoy doing?

- Since I may have more time in retirement, what can I do now?

This chapter will help you seek God's purpose for your life by offering another inventory for your use. We saw the first one in the chapter 2, Tool B: Spiritual Gifts Inventory. If you haven't had a chance to complete it, go ahead and do it now. Even if you have taken a spiritual gifts inventory in the past, take it again at this stage in your life. You may make a new discovery. The second, located at the end of this chapter, is Tool C: Crossroads Inventory to help manifest the big picture on how you can bring meaning to the second half of your life.

The Crossroads Inventory covers seven essential questions to better understand your unique God-given and essential purpose in life:

What are your **s**piritual gifts?

What are your abilities?

What time and financial resources can you offer?

What makes you unique?

What are your dreams?

What can you learn from your past that can help you now?

What can you do now that you could not do before?

There are lifetime benefits for knowing your personal portfolio and purpose as you grow through the various stages of retirement. See Tool C: Crossroads Inventory for worksheets.

Mike's Story

(As told by Pastor Clayton Smith)

Before Mike relocated, he was a well-known and respected community leader. He served as the lay leader in his church and the president of his university alumni council, and he practiced law in private practice before becoming a federal prosecuting attorney. Seeking justice and being a lawyer was something Mike had wanted to do since the seventh grade. Service was central to Mike and to his wife, Donna.

Together, they were blessed with family and many friends in this university community. I know all this about Mike and Donna because I served as their pastor for eight years in the wonderful community of Cape Girardeau, Missouri (population 40,000). Mike taught my daughter and son in high school church classes. Mike, like Nehemiah, has the spiritual gift of leadership. I am so pleased that I now continue to be their pastor and friend in Kansas City.

While Mike and Donna were living in Cape Girardeau, their two married sons and four grandchildren lived in Kansas City, seven hours away. That's why it did not surprise me when, on the first day of Mike's retirement from the federal government, they left their hometown and their congregation of more than fifty years to begin a new adventure. I welcomed them to Kansas City and to our church, as I had made the same move three years earlier.

Mike now reports that his career in the practice of law taught him several lessons that prepared them for a meaningful retirement, one of which was that family was their first priority. They were willing to say good-bye to their community status, security, and the satisfaction that comes with the respect of many friends. They had both been successful in their active roles in the community and church service for God and country.

Mike and Donna have now been retired for more than seven years. Retirement offered a new challenge and opportunities to serve God and others. They have more time for each other, for their children and grandchildren, and for their many new friends. Mike is excited about building memories with his grandchildren. He and Donna have discovered that it is much easier and lots more fun to be grandparents than parents!

They feel less pressure and have noticed better health with more time to exercise. They joined a new adult church class and Mike served as their class mission project coordinator. He now serves Church of the Resurrection's Church partner team as a coach for New Horizons UMC in Columbia, Missouri. He has greater energy for more activities in retirement than he did during his professional career.

Since Mike graduated from law school in Kansas City, he also has opportunities to mentor young law students. The privilege of serving God and country continues to be a priority that he shares with others. His purpose and self-discipline in life was formed while playing high school and college football. He also learned the value of sacrifice serving his country in the Army, where he was stationed in Vietnam.

Retirement has transformed Mike and Donna's lives. Now they are transforming the lives of others, especially their grandchildren! They don't have the community status they once had when Mike was a federal prosecuting attorney, but many new relationships seem to have deeper significance and satisfaction. They don't live their lives around the rigid work schedule as they did for forty years. They do have flexibility to travel and find more freedom to follow their dreams. When I asked Mike if he had an idea about how God was using his gifts, passions, and energy, he gave me a list of more than twenty ways he found joy in serving. He really knows how to make a difference!

I hope you know someone like Mike. I have admired Mike and Donna for nearly twenty years. They have all the qualities of servant leaders. At the heart of Christian ministry is the outreaching love of God and others. Those who are always seeking a higher purpose express the mind and mission of Christ by demonstrating gratitude and devotion to God.

Questions for Discussion

1. What are the key elements for this story?

_____

_____

_____

2. How do you relate to this story?

_____

_____

_____

3. What are the next steps you could take?

_____

_____

_____

Understanding the Bible Story

Read Nehemiah 1. Nehemiah was a servant to the King Artaxerxes during the exile of the nation of Judah. One of his brothers came back from Judah to report distressing news about Jerusalem.

Have you ever mourned? Describe your body, mind, and soul at that time.

_____

_____

_____

Look at the different parts of Nehemiah's prayer. What is the first action Nehemiah takes?

_____

_____

_____

Why is confession a key part of prayer?

_____

_____

_____

In his prayer, how does Nehemiah describe God, and what God did? Why is it vital to believe that God can accomplish what you are asking?

_____

_____

_____

_____

Why do you think Nehemiah reminds God that he has been praying day and night?

_____

_____

_____

> *Please give success to your servant today and grant*
> *him favor in the presence of this man!*
>
> *—Nehemiah 1:11*

Read Nehemiah 2. Nehemiah involved the one man who could make things move forward, the king. Nehemiah thought out his plan and identified the time it would take, the materials needed, and the necessity of the king's written blessing. When Nehemiah journeys to Jerusalem, he demonstrates how to be a leader in ministry.

Why did Nehemiah seek the king's blessing?

_____

_____

_____

How did he attack Jerusalem's problems? Identify his steps. What did he do first? How did he evaluate his chances of rebuilding Jerusalem's wall?

_____

_____

_____

> *What fills the heart comes out of the mouth.*
>
> *—Matthew 12:34b*

Small Group Discussion Questions

How did Nehemiah involve his head, heart, and hands in the rebuilding of Jerusalem's wall?

_____

_____

_____

Have you ever fasted from food or other activities? Describe your experience. How did it draw you closer to God?

_____

_____

_____

In his prayer, Nehemiah claimed promises God had made. Name some of the promises God has made to you.

_____

_____

_____

How can Nehemiah's story help you formulate a plan for retirement?

_____

_____

_____

Why do you need a plan in place before you transition into retirement?

_____

_____

_____

And serve each other according to the gift each person has received...

—1 Peter 4:10

Experiencing Your Life Story

As you seek God's purpose for your life, you begin to see the big picture. There is a fine art in seeing the long view. This is called wisdom! Now is the time to imagine all God wants you to be.

> *Halftime is a pause in midlife to reflect on what we have accomplished, who we have become, and what will matter in the end. It is a point to redirect our time and resources for the second half.*
>
> —*Bob Buford,* Halftime

Pray and reflect on the seven activities listed below.

- Read and reflect on scripture.
- Be open to personal insights from God and other people. As you identify, define, and claim your gifts and abilities for ministry, you may find that your characteristics have changed and matured over time.
- Do a self-assessment based on your experiences. In the past, what brought you the greatest sense of meaning and joy at different stages of your life? Examine common threads to see what you loved or still love to do.
- Seek the counsel of a pastor or trusted friend.
- Realize that one of the best ways to learn is by doing. Trial and error will be the best teacher.

Each of you can make heartfelt strides in the second half of your life. Look at your individual descriptions. Do not compare yourself to others. When you believe you are fulfilling God's purpose and following God's will, you are able to act from a sense of freedom to be and do what fits you best. This produces great satisfaction and greater glory to God.

The writer of Hebrews prays that God will "equip you with every good thing to do [God's] will, / by developing in us what pleases [God] through Jesus Christ" (Heb

13:21). When you align your desires with God's purpose for you, God is faithful to equip you to do the work.

Once you identify and understand your strengths, you can better apply them in service to others in retirement—or at any stage in life. Most people who have had successful careers utilized their strengths in daily work. In this transitional season of life, these strengths can move you from success in your career to significance in retirement. In the next chapter, you will learn how to develop your purpose into a personal, spiritually based strategic plan.

⊷ Tool C ⊷
CROSSROADS INVENTORY

Your Crossroads Map

Discover the most significant ways you can know, love, and serve God in your retirement. This is your personal and confidential guide. Remember that your season of life will affect how you answer the inventory. Many people discover that their spiritual gifts have changed in the second half of their lives. You will want to learn from this inventory so that you can find places to serve in the second half of life that will bring you joy and significance.

What are your spiritual gifts?

Top two spiritual gifts I believe I have:

1. _____

2. _____

What are your abilities, talents, and skills?

My current/past vocation is:

_____

Other jobs or skills I have experience in:

_____

_____

_____

_____

I feel I have these specialized talents:

_____

_____

_____

_____

I have taught a class or led a seminar on:

_____

_____

_____

I feel my most valuable personal ability/talent is:

_____

_____

_____

What time and financial resources can you offer?

How would I best manage my time in retirement?

_____ For self

_____ For family

_____ For others

Whom do I want to touch and impact?

_____ Neighbors

_____ Strangers

_____ Local or international

_____ Age level(s)

What is something new I would like to do?

_____

_____

What financial resources will I have to share?

_____ My tithe

_____ My offerings

_____ My legacy

| **What makes you unique and capable?** |

Personality—This is how I see myself.

Where do I tend to get my energy and ideas? From myself or from others?

_____

How do I tend to receive information? Through my senses or through intuition?

_____

How do I tend to process information? Through my feelings or through thinking it out?

_____

What kind of lifestyle do I prefer? Planned/routine or spontaneous/variety?

_____

Sphere of Service—Prioritize how you prefer to serve (rank in order 1-4).

_____ Organizational (structured/ongoing)
_____ Projects (periodic/short term)
_____ Promptings (spontaneous/personal)
_____ Risk-taking (try something new/different)

Expression—Prioritize how you prefer to express your care for others (rank in order 1-5).

_____ Words of affirmation
_____ Quality time
_____ Personal contact/interaction
_____ Acts of service
_____ Gift giving

| **What are your desires and passions?** |

What motivates me?
    To serve God?

_____

    To work?

_____

    To study?

_____

With whom or on what do I most love to work? (focus of work)

1. People
2. Projects
3. Information
4. Ideas
5. Causes
6. Other

Church mission, ministries, or possible needs that I have a passion for serving:

1. _____
2. _____
3. _____

What can you learn from your past and present? What can you do NOW that you could not do before?

Spiritual Experiences

This is how and when I became a Christian and what it has meant to me since then:

_____
_____
_____
_____
_____
_____
_____

Describe your level of spiritual growth.

_____ Seeker—I'm investigating Christianity.

_____ New/Young believer—I recently became a Christian.

_____ Stable/Growing believer—I am actively pursuing Christ.

_____ Leading/Guiding believer—I am able to model faithfulness, inspire and guide others, and lead by example.

Educational Experiences

When I was attending school my favorite subjects were:

_____

_____

_____

Topics or subject matter I tend to gravitate toward:

_____

_____

_____

Seminars or training that have been meaningful to me:

_____

_____

_____

Family/Relational Experiences

What kind of situations in my family life or with other relationships could I relate to with other Christians?

_____

_____

_____

_____

Painful Experiences

What kinds of trials, problems, or difficulties have I experienced that I could relate to with fellow Christians?

_____

_____

_____

_____

Vocational Experiences

Employment opportunities I have had that could relate to other Christians:

_____

_____

_____

Ministry Experiences

Where have I served in the past?

Name of church(es)

_____

Area(s) of service

_____

Position(s) of service

_____

Years of service

_____

Mission Experiences

What kinds of mission projects (local, national, and international) have I participated in that would prepare me for other mission project opportunities?

_____

_____

_____

_____

Worship Experiences

What kind of worship style(s) do I prefer?

_____

_____

What group(s) do I want to serve?

____infants ____children ____youth ____young adults ____adults

____55+ ____senior adults ____ people of any age with disabilities

How can I best know, love, and serve God?

I feel I am best suited for the following types of ministries to make a significant difference and enduring impact:

1. _____

2. _____

3. _____

4. _____

What additional questions do I now have?

_____

_____

_____

Do I want to meet with a pastor or staff member for more information on preparing for the second half of my life?

_____

If so, with whom?

_____

Chapter 4
JOY FOR THE JOURNEY

Scripture Verse

Just be very careful to carry out the commandment and Instruction that Moses the LORD's servant commanded you. Love the LORD your God. Walk in all his ways and obey his commandments. Hold on to him and serve him with all your heart and being.

—*Joshua 22:5*

Opening Prayer

Holy Spirit, our gentle guide, give us strength and perseverance to keep pace with you as we move into this new time of our lives. You commission each believer to go into the world and make disciples. You promise to be with us always. Thank you. Amen.

> *Jesus said to them, "I am fed by doing the will of the one who sent me and by completing his work."*
>
> —*John 4:34*

Introduction

Retirement is a time to discover other things you can do by pushing boundaries. Ken Robinson writes in *The Element: How Finding Your Passion Changes Everything* that "the only way to prepare for the future is to make the most out of ourselves on the assumption that doing so will make us as flexible and productive as possible."[1] Retirement can be a time to turn your life in a new direction spiritually or grab ahold of God-given opportunities that you once missed.

People who have successfully transitioned from employment to retirement believe they still have much to learn and want to have fun along the way. They retire *to* something, not *from* something, and they have plans in place before retirement starts, plans that give them a future with hope.

Getting to Know You

What attributes did you discover about yourself from completing the Tool C: Crossroads Inventory?

How will knowing, loving, and serving God through your church, family, and community enrich you and the second half of your life?

Will You Have a Purpose-Filled Second Half of Life?

This chapter focuses on developing a spiritually significant purpose statement for the second half of your life. This statement will drive your choices each day toward leading a purpose-filled retirement right now and in the future.

A personal God-directed mission statement will serve as a life guide regardless of your age, career, stage of retirement, abilities, or dreams. Everything you decide to do will be measured by whether it fulfills God's purpose for your life. If you already have a life mission statement, update it as you enter retirement to add value and productivity to the second half of your life.

> *We know that God works all things together for good for the ones who love God, for those who are called according to his purpose.*
>
> *—Romans 8:28*

Paul's Story

(As told by Dave Wilson)

Paul retired as an executive of a nationally known baking company. He spent his entire forty-three-year business career at one company, where he just kept being promoted. Paul had a number of key reasons for his success; one was that he mixed well with people. Another was that he was tireless. He got up early and left late and put in a half-day on Saturday just to get things done.

Upon retiring, his goal was to keep busy, to do something. One of his busy works was taking care of his yard. I have seen Paul's yard and can truly say it is fantastic, but Paul will tell you that yard work grew boring. He hung around the house so much that his wife, Shirley, told him that she married him for better or for worse, but not for lunch. She also kept asking him what he was going to do *now*.

Paul needed to make a decision: either sit on his rear and watch TV, or do something significant. Shirley was and still is active in church. She decided to find something for him to do there to serve others. She found the church's food drive and Paul helped. One thing led to another, Paul started assisting other ways, and people learned quickly that he would take care of what needed to be done. He discovered he had the spiritual gift of helping.

Over the past several years, Paul involved himself in several of the church's key outreach programs. He helped head the Bless the School Program in which the church refurbished inner-city schools with new playgrounds on the outside and new paint on the inside. This ministry to the inner city led Paul to be involved in another program that sent backpacks home with kids who did not have enough to eat over the weekends during the school year. Each week volunteers pack and distribute backpacks to children in six inner-city schools with whom the church now collaborates.

Today Paul is heavily involved in the church's Furnishings Ministry to people who can't afford bedding and furniture. As when he worked for a living, Paul continues to get up early and stay late, but he does this with what he calls "Christian responsibility." Every day he is excited to go meet people, get to know them, and help meet their needs.

Paul's mission statement is short and straight to the point: To help others and do it.

1. What are the key elements to Paul's story?

_____

_____

_____

2. How do you relate to Paul's story?

_____

_____

_____

3. What steps will you take next?

_____

_____

_____

Understanding the Bible Story

Read John 4:34-38. Jesus starts to teach his disciples about living in service to God. The Samaritan woman at the well has left to tell everyone she knew about the man she had just met. Now the entire town of Sychar is coming out to meet Jesus. Jesus teaches his disciples the principle that doing God's work brings joy. Look at what the Bible teaches about living with joy in service to God.

How have you received sown seeds of joy?

_____

How have you received the seeds of joy from others?

_____

What are the blessings and joys that you receive from serving others?

_____

Read Proverbs 7:1-5. Proverbs 7 portrays wisdom and folly (sinfulness) as two different women.

What does wisdom require you to do?

_____

_____

_____

What does it mean to write wisdom's teachings on your heart?

_____

_____

_____

Read Ecclesiastes 3. Tradition says that the Teacher was King Solomon. God inspired him to tell us that there is a time and place for everything in life. In other words, God is a God of order, not chaos.

How does God ask you to manage your time in Ecclesiastes 3:12-13?

_____

_____

_____

Take a weekly calendar and fill it out with how you now spend your time, including e-mail, social media websites, phone calls, favorite television shows, eating, sleeping, exercise, and other activities and appointments. What do you notice about it after you fill it out?

_____

_____

_____

Make a list of activities on which you would like to spend your time (some might be the same as you do now). What is different between the two lists?

_____

_____

_____

A personal strategic plan with godly priorities and great organization will enable you to do even more than you imagine. The secret, as the Teacher says in Ecclesiastes 3:1, is to remember "There's a season for everything / and a time for every matter under the heavens."

> *"If I, your Lord and Teacher, have washed your feet, you too must wash each other's feet. I have given you an example: Just as I have done, you also must do."*
>
> —*John 13:14-15*

Read 1 Timothy 6:5-19. What aspects of managing one's purpose does Paul give to Timothy?

_____

_____

_____

Small Group Discussion Questions

How do you define joy? Where do you find joy?

_____

_____

_____

What robs you of your joy?

_____

_____

_____

How do you define inspiration?

_____

_____

_____

Who or what inspires you?

_____

_____

_____

How do you define success? How do you define significance? Which is better: success or significance?

_____

_____

_____

What have you learned from scripture about having a spiritually significant purpose?

_____

_____

_____

> *This above all: to thine own self be true. And it must follow, as the night the day, thou canst not then be false to any man.*
>
> —*Shakespeare*, Hamlet

Experiencing Your Life Story

Writing your spiritually significant personal mission statement is the next step in developing a retirement plan. Mission statements are not just for corporations or high-level executives. Whether you are a stay-at-home mom, a retail store manager, a college student, or a truck driver, crafting a personal mission statement focuses you on meeting your long-term goals. It serves as a guidepost for how you will find greater impact in life. The cost of a mission statement is small, but the outcome is great because it works!

Tool D: Mission/Purpose Statement at the end of this chapter can help you work through the process of creating a mission/purpose statement to navigate the second half of your life.

> *Many plans are in a person's mind, / but the LORD's purpose will succeed.*
>
> —*Proverbs 19:21*

Write a Draft of Your Personal Mission Statement

1. First, pray. This will lay the foundation for constructing a purpose statement. Ask God what God's purpose is for your life (Jer 29:11). Thank God for giving you gifts of time, talent, and resources and for giving you a purpose and a future with hope.

2. Take time to think through your answers in the Tool C: Crossroads Inventory at the end of chapter 3.

3. In fifty words or less, write a first draft of your mission statement for the rest of your life. Don't worry if your statement isn't similar to your friend's or spouse's. Every statement is different because no two people are the same.

First Draft Mission Statement:

_____

_____

_____

_____

_____

_____

_____

_____

4. Add your personal and spiritual values that you already live by. (For example, love the Lord with all your heart, soul, mind, and strength, and love your neighbor as yourself.)

Top Three Values to Live by:

a. _____

b. _____

c. _____

> *Think about the things above and not things on earth.*
>
> *—Colossians 3:2*

5. Start using your mission statement. Write it down. Memorize it. Frame it. Put a copy where you will see it every day. Repeat it to yourself each morning. When trying to decide if you should do something, ask yourself how that activity will fulfill your mission.

6. For those who want to develop a strategic planning process in much greater detail, please use Tool E: Planning Checklist (at the end of this chapter) to help you identify areas of interest, experience, or curiosity in how you plan to use your time and resources in the second half of your life. Then go to Tool F: Writing a Strategic Plan to describe critical issues, goals, and action steps you will take. This S.M.A.R.T. (Significant, Meaningful, Altruistic, Realistic, and Timely) planning model is derived from the business world. It can also serve you well in the second half of your life!

━━ Tool D ━━
Mission/Purpose Statement

Do You Have a Mission/Purpose Statement?

Mission statements are for everyone. It is important to prepare your mission statement to help you navigate the second half of your life.

Begin by asking the right questions:

1. How will you define your purpose?

2. Who do you want to be?

3. What is on your bucket list to do for yourself and others?

4. What skills and abilities do you bring?

5. Where do you want to get involved?

6. Whom do you want to help?

7. What other questions should you ask yourself?

Time management and financial resources will have specific impact on what you do for yourself and others. Make a schedule and budget for each month, so every day can count. You might begin with a three-month plan.

Ask: What is God's purpose for my life? Use the following scriptures as a guide.

1. "Many are the plans in a person's mind, / but the Lord's *purpose* will succeed" (Prov 19:21, emphasis added).

2. "We know that God works all things together for good for the ones who love God, for those who are called according to his purpose" (Rom 8:28).

Step One: List Personal and Spiritual Values

Identify your personal values and spiritual beliefs that will sustain all that you do and will become a legacy for those you love.

1.
2.
3.
4.

Step Two: List Your Top Two Spiritual Gifts

1.
2.

Step Three: Write Your Mission/Purpose Statement

Prepare your first draft. Pray and think about what will bring you the greatest significance and joy. Write it again and again until you have a brief statement. Make it something that you can easily remember.

Mission/Purpose Statement:

_____

_____

_____

_____

_____

_____

Having your purpose written out will add value and joy to your second half of life. Do it now! Share your mission statement with others who can give you feedback. You want other key people in your life to support you and your new lifestyle.

PLANNING CHECKLIST

The following checklist can help you identify areas of interest, experience, or curiosity in how you plan to use your time and resources in the second half of your life. This list is a guide; you may have many more areas you wish to explore or include in your second half of life. Please check your priorities in the following list:

Faith

_____ Study
_____ Worship
_____ Service
_____ Fellowship
_____ Generosity
_____ Spiritual growth

Family/Friends Relationship

_____ Children
_____ Grandchildren
_____ Extended family (parents, siblings, other relatives)
_____ New friends
_____ Longtime friends
_____ Coworkers/former coworkers

Lifelong Learning

_____ Classes at church
_____ Classes at university, community college

_____ Mental sharpness (e-learning, crossword puzzles, dancing, etc.)
_____ Moral/ethical development

Health

_____ Preventive care
_____ Medical care
_____ Insurance costs
_____ Medications
_____ Reality diet
_____ Health directives
_____ Exercise options

Financial

_____ Annual budget/spending plan
_____ Available savings
_____ Investments
_____ Conservative/risk factors
_____ Cost of living
_____ Social Security
_____ Money sharks/scams to avoid
_____ Donations to church and charity
_____ Estate planning

Where to Live?

_____ Near family
_____ Near friends
_____ Retirement locations
_____ Retirement communities
_____ Multiple locations

Community Involvement

_____ Civic clubs
_____ Political causes

_____ Sports
_____ Schools, libraries
_____ Historical societies
_____ Gardening clubs

Hobbies

_____ Personal
_____ Group
_____ Seasonal

Travel

_____ Short/long trips
_____ Timeshares
_____ Tourist traps
_____ Traveling with groups/tours
_____ Traveling alone
_____ Where to travel, places to see

Mentoring

_____ Spiritual mentoring
_____ Professional
_____ Family
_____ Friends
_____ K-12 students in public schools

Time Management

_____ Family time
_____ Quiet time for prayer, Bible study, meditation
_____ Full-time work
_____ Part-time work

_____ Volunteer work

_____ Church

_____ Community

Legacy

_____ Percentage model/dollar amounts

_____ Completing your will or trust

_____ Family

_____ Church

_____ Charity

_____ Heirlooms

_____ Journal or life history/highlights

_____ Words of thanks to family and friends

_____ Values/how do you want to be remembered?

Dying Well

_____ Guardianships

_____ Power of attorney

_____ Health directives

_____ Plans for your memorial service/written funeral requests

_____ A written blessing for others

Writing a Strategic Plan

Once you establish your mission statement, consider how you will fulfill it. This is not a to-do list, but a strategic way to realize your mission. The mission statement is central to every strategic plan. You must be able to articulate clearly your God-directed purpose, your reason for being. The word *strategic* means a plan that guides your entire life, a plan that allows you to carry out your mission and achieve your goals.

Look at the critical issues in your life, those challenges to your mission and life-style that could be critical to your success in the second half of your life. Most people have some of the following issues:

- Health
- Faith
- Finances
- Personal Safety
- Family
- Social/environmental/political
- Transportation

You may have other critical issues. Address these issues in your strategic plan. As other issues arise, they too can be added to your plan.

To organize your plan, answer the following questions.

- What are your goals in the second half of your life? These goals spell out what the future results you hope to achieve. Be specific. How do these goals incorporate the critical issues you previously identified?
- What do you need to do to achieve your goals? When do you want to achieve these goals; what is your schedule? What needs to be done first? What is the next step?

- What resources do you have to accomplish your goals? What other people need to be involved?

- What are your capabilities? (See Tool B: Spiritual Gifts Inventory in chapter 2.) What are the implications for family and friends and for your lifestyle?

- What do you want to accomplish within the next year? Within five years?

Worksheet 1: Identifying Critical Issues, Goals, and Action Steps (Example)

Critical Issues

1. Spiritual Growth

Goals

Goal 1: To grow in my understanding of God
Attainment (when, who, resources)
    When: Over the next year (12 months)
    Who: Pastor, family, friends
    Resources:

- Weekly worship services

- Other church programs

- Small group Bible study weekly

- Sunday school classes

- Mission trips, service projects, church website

Actions I Can Take

- Attend weekly worship. Take notes on sermon and meditate on notes throughout the week. Follow Grow, Pray, and Study daily lesson. Respond to call to action.

- Participate in a FaithWorks Saturday activity each month.

- Call the church to learn about classes, small groups, and service opportunities.

- Join a weekly class that studies the Bible.

- Pray daily.

- Take a class on prayer.

- Ask a pastor to help me find and meet with a spiritual growth mentor.

- Avoid situations that will detract from my Bible study and spiritual growth.

- Prioritize my time to be about God and communicating with God.

Worksheet 1: Identifying Your Critical Issues, Goals, and Action Steps

Fill in the following outline according to your plans. Identify your critical issues, set goals, and then determine the strategies and actions you can take to achieve your goal.

Critical Issues

1. _____
2. _____
3. _____
4. _____

Goal 1:

Attainment: Be Specific, Measurable, Altruistic, Realistic, Timely
When:

_____

_____

Who:

_____

_____

Resources:

_____

_____

Actions I Can Take

_____

_____

_____

Goal 2:

Attainment: Be Specific, Measurable, Altruistic, Realistic, Timely
When:

_____

_____

Who:

_____

_____

Resources:

_____

_____

Actions I Can Take

_____

_____

_____

Goal 3:

Attainment: Be Specific, Measurable, Altruistic, Realistic, Timely
When:

_____

_____

Who:

_____

_____

Resources:

_____

_____

Actions I Can Take

_____

_____

_____

You may have fewer goals for your retirement plan, but no more than three; otherwise, the plan becomes difficult to achieve.

Worksheet 2: Implementing Your Spiritually Significant Plan for Navigating the Second Half of Your Life

To make sure you actually use your plan, complete the following worksheet. Address each critical issue on a separate sheet of paper and then combine them into your final spiritually significant plan for navigating the second half of your life.

Most of us have trouble knowing what to say to family and friends about decisions we want to make for the second half of our lives. This happens especially when we do not have a clear and concise plan. Review your mission statement to see if you can answer the following questions. The following strategic planning model derived from the business realm can give some direction:

- **S**ignificant—What are your goals that will bring more joy?
- **M**eaningful—What will bring great purpose to others?
- **A**ltruistic—What resources are necessary to bless others?
- **R**ealistic—What are the implications for family and friends?
- **T**imely—What do you want your legacy to be?

When you develop your plan and then implement it in the second half of life, good things begin to happen.

Critical Issue

_____

_____

_____

What I want to accomplish:

_____

_____

Actions I will take to achieve this goal (include time, resources, and people):

_____

_____

How often will I evaluate where I am in achieving my goal?

_____

_____

_____

Chapter 5

CARING CONVERSATIONS WITH FAMILY AND FRIENDS

Scripture Verse

But if someone doesn't provide for their own family, and especially for a member of their household, they have denied the faith. They are worse than those who have no faith.

—1 Timothy 5:8

Opening Prayer

Creator of heaven and earth and our creator too, thank you for the people you have put into our lives. They have helped to make us the people we are today. Give us the words to say when talking with our family and friends about planning for the future. Only you know what will come tomorrow. We pray in the name of your son, our Lord Jesus. Amen.

Introduction

Planning for your retirement years can be one of the most creative and constructive experiences of your life. Just as you planned where to go to college, which job to take, and where to move, you want to plan the second half of life with similar diligence and enthusiasm. God wants you to be all that you can be. God loves you completely and calls you to finish your life well. Getting older may change your concept of self, but in no way discounts the vital impact of living fully every day.

63

It is important to prepare now for the second half of life by talking with your families and close friends. The scriptures lift up the value of families and friends and especially the priority of keeping family in mind as you plan for your retirement years. Involve your family as you think about what you want to do, where you want to live, and how you want to make a difference. With whom do you need to have a caring conversation?

In Tool G: Caring Conversations at the end of this chapter you will find a helpful resource. If you involve your close family and friends in caring conversations about your retirement, you will honor them, learn from them, and benefit by the conversations. Family is important. Later in life when you may need to have conversations about more difficult end-of-life decisions you will find that because you have already involved your family in retirement planning other conversations will be much easier and more natural.

Getting to Know You

Please share your personal mission statement.

What did you learn as you went through the process of writing your spiritual mission statement for retirement?

> *Everything God does is purposeful. And since God is in each of us, each of us has a purpose.*
>
> —*Iyanla Vanzant, life coach*[1]

Will You Have a Purpose-Filled Second Half of Life?

You learn a lot from conversations with significant others in your life, yet too often you forget to talk with those you love the most about significant matters in planning for the second half of your life. This chapter will underscore the importance of sharing your stories and learning from others. Thoughtful conversations with family and friends can be encouraging. You can share your dreams and visions and invite others to share theirs. When everyone is informed and involved, better decisions are made. Just as you remind yourself that you have unique spiritual gifts and abilities, remember too that you have unique relationships.

Our Western contemporary culture today tries to hide the reality of aging and puts emphasis on youth and vitality. In contrast to this worldly culture, Christian faith teaches how to live with physical limitations and unlimited wisdom. As one of God's people, your fears about aging fade and your faith expands when the Holy Spirit works to help you become more Christlike.

> *The fruit of the Spirit is love, joy, peace, patience, kindness, goodness, faithfulness, gentleness, and self-control. There is no law against things like this.*
>
> *—Galatians 5:22-23*

Myron's Story

(As told by Dave Wilson)

Myron started his medical career in Family Practice, then moved to emergency medicine after four years, then moved to Urgent Care. He didn't like caring for people on an ongoing basis. He preferred Urgent Care because he could see patients briefly and then "get rid of them." By his own portrayal, he was not a pleasant man.

Myron, a functioning alcoholic, loved to eat. When he retired at age fifty-nine, Myron weighed more than three hundred pounds. He viewed retirement as an end to his medical career; it excited him that he would never see patients again. Myron had no good plan for retirement; he just wanted to be loose and reckless. He didn't have a church and spent his time following college baseball and drinking each night.

In 2003, Myron and his wife, Joyce, moved to Kansas City. They decided that some things needed to change, and they found a small church where they liked the pastor.

Myron was still overeating and drinking when his brother died of a cardiac arrest while playing in a bridge tournament. Even though he was not close to his brother, the death had two significant impacts upon his and Joyce's lives. First, they joined

Weight Watchers. Realizing that more than half of his caloric intake was in alcohol, he made the decision to stop drinking on January 4, 2004. They then spent time working with Weight Watchers.

The second item that affected them, especially Joyce, was how the faith community of Myron's sister-in-law cared for her. Joyce noted her church had provided grief care and began to wonder what she would have done for similar care had the death been Myron's. Even though she was reasonably satisfied with the small church they had found, Joyce started attending studies and events at the United Methodist Church of the Resurrection. After some time Myron began to attend with her. It was close to their home and they liked the feel of the place. It wasn't long until Myron's life really began to change. He took an Alpha Class and joined a small group study of the Gospel of Mark where the group opened in prayer. They even prayed in pairs with each other. Myron had never prayed for another person before that time, privately or anywhere. Myron was somewhat scared at first, yet found it inviting. He did not last long. After this study, he joined a Disciple Bible study group, and that really got his attention. He also discovered that prayer was not frightening at all.

In 2007, he responded to a notice about a new program that the church was developing to help pastors care for people in the congregation. Volunteer Congregational Care Ministers (CCM) serve in prayer, shepherding, teaching, visiting, and performing many other tasks to help the ordained pastors. Myron thought that perhaps this would keep him occupied. He completed the CCM training requirements, and the church assigned him to a CCM team. Myron still had no thoughts or interest in dealing with people again. The pastor he worked with had other ideas regarding what his duties would be.

Starting out, Myron had two experiences that truly changed his life. He physically experienced a heart-warming feeling about the work to be done and asked one of the pastors what she thought about it. She said it was obviously an encounter with the Holy Spirit. Myron asked what that meant and her answer was, "You'll find out." Shortly afterward, he was asked to make two hospital visits. He reminded the pastor that he didn't like seeing patients. Her reply was, "That is not an appropriate answer to the question I asked. I asked, 'Will you go?'" He went to the hospital, but didn't pray with either patient, and hurried back to his car. In the car, he heard a very clear voice telling him that he had been given some great gifts to share and that his performance was not very pleasing. God wanted Myron to use those gifts. Shaken by the experience, Myron now knew what he was to do and made the decision to do it.

In the past six years, Myron has become a blessing and an inspiration to many. He has been relentless in prayer and caring for others in crisis situations. Myron himself admitted that "for most of my life I was not a nice person." Now he inspires an entire church with his kind words and attention to others' needs. His second half of life has, indeed, been one of significance!

Questions for Discussion

What are the key elements of Myron's story?

_____

_____

_____

How do you relate to his story?

_____

_____

_____

What are the next steps for you to take?

_____

_____

_____

Understanding the Bible Story

Jesus had many caring conversations with his friends during meals, while walking along a road, and at other times throughout the day. The most poignant ones occurred the night before he was arrested and crucified.

Read John 16:23-33. How did Jesus prepare his disciples for the future?

_____

_____

_____

_____

What do you learn from the passage that you can apply to conversations you want to have with the people who care about you?

_____

_____

_____

Read Genesis 47:28-31 and 49:1-2. When he was about 130 years old, Jacob traveled to Egypt and reunited with his son, Joseph. Jacob was old, but lived in Egypt another seventeen years. He wanted to relay information to all his sons.

Describe the conversations Jacob (Israel) had with his sons.

_____

_____

_____

What do you learn from Jacob's conversations that you can apply to your retirement plans?

_____

_____

_____

Read Romans 12:4-8. How do these verses emphasize unity within diversity?

_____

_____

_____

What do you learn about spiritual gifts that might influence your conversations with family and friends?

_____

_____

_____

Small Group Discussion Questions

Have you thought about ways you might bless your family members and friends?

_____

_____

_____

How do you feel about having conversations with people close to you about your plans for your second half of life, including end-of-life decisions and financial arrangements?

_____

_____

_____

What might your family, trusted friends, and advisors bring to your retirement planning?

_____

_____

_____

Experiencing Your Life Story

In the last chapter, you developed a mission statement to guide your decisions in planning a spiritually significant retirement. As part of your planning, include family members, trusted friends, and counselors. They will be affected by your plans for the next season of life. Many of them have a stake in you and your plans. Recall from the first chapter of this study the following:

- Retirement is about the significant difference you can make.

- It is about your opportunity to change lives.

- It is about your impact on family, friends, church, and community.

- It is about leaving a sustaining legacy for those you love.

The following are just a few topics for conversations you can have with family and friends:

- Family and personal relationships

- Spiritual and religious values

- End-of-life decisions

- Legal decisions

- Financial decisions

- Health care advance directive

A more comprehensive list of two dozen subjects can be found in Tool G: Caring Conversations at the end of this chapter.

> *We have different gifts that are consistent with God's grace that has been given to us. If your gift is prophecy, you should prophesy in proportion to your faith. If you gift is service, devote yourself to serving. If your gift is teaching, devote yourself to teaching. If your gift is encouragement, devote yourself to encouraging. The one giving should do it with no strings attached. The leader should lead with passion. The one showing mercy should be cheerful.*
>
> *—Romans 12:6-8*

You may have trouble knowing what to say to family and friends about decisions you want to make for the second half of your life. This is a common discomfort. People often avoid conversations about values and faith, particularly when they are centered on what happens in the future.

In the same way, families circumvent discussions about when to take away driving privileges, long-term care arrangements, and health problems that might compromise quality of life. As difficult as these conversations are—even Jesus's disciples didn't want him to talk about "going away"—when you develop plans with input from family members, friends, and advisors, you will enjoy peace and so will they.

You can learn from others who are experiencing a fulfilling second half of life. Most report that they find ways to nurture their mind, heart, and soul. Take time to ask people you respect about how they find significance in their lives. You may find that you can make the most of life when you do the following:

- Learn and value better coping skills.
- Value wisdom over physical power and good looks.
- Love others.
- Reach out to people of all ages/stages.
- Discover a variety of religious experiences.

- Define yourself by who you are, not what you do.
- Transcend physical limitations.
- Celebrate faith, hope, and love.
- Develop artistic appreciation (music, art, etc.).

The second half of life also can bring significant moral growth. By growing spiritually, you can have a significant impact on your community, church, and country. Read Romans 12:9-21 and consider the ways you can accomplish justice and extend compassion by

- honoring others above yourself;
- serving others;
- advocating for the needs of others;
- being joyful in hope, patient in affliction, and faithful in prayer;
- sharing with God's people who are in need; and
- practicing hospitality.

Here are a few other ways to be intentional about your spiritual growth:

- Live what you believe.
- Pray for others.
- Study the Bible.
- Serve as spiritual guides/care ministers.
- Teach spiritual truths/coaching.
- Worship and celebrate all of God's blessings.
- Discover stages of spiritual growth.
- Read scriptures and great books.

◆ Tool G ◆
CARING CONVERSATIONS

We learn a lot from conversations with those special and significant others in our lives. Too often, we forget to have caring conversations with those we love the most about such significant matters in planning for the second half of our lives. We want to underscore the importance of sharing our stories. You may want to write your story down to become something of your memoir for future generations.

Family First

It is vitally important to prepare for the second half of life by talking first with our families. The scriptures lift up the value of families and especially the priority of keeping your family in mind as you plan for your retirement years.

First Timothy 5:8 stresses the responsibility of putting family first in this way: "But if someone doesn't provide for their own family, and especially for a member of their household, they have denied the faith. They are worse than those who have no faith."

Caring conversations with family and friends can be encouraging. You can share your dreams and visions! When everyone is informed and involved, the decisions are positive and beneficial to all. Too often, these important decisions are made without thinking about what you do best in life. You need to remind yourself that you have unique spiritual gifts and abilities to share with those you love. You are called to lead with your best gifts and personal strengths.

Caring conversations with family can also be very difficult. It is important to first discuss your plans for the second half of your life journey. When you do this well, you can then begin to talk about your health care wishes and even end-of-life issues.

For most of us, the best way to have these conversations is by writing down the key points we want to communicate. After having the conversation, we can then give the written instructions to our family.

The following are just a few of the areas for caring conversations:

- Family and personal relationships
- Spiritual and religious values
- Legacy gifts
- End-of-life decisions
- Legal decisions
- Financial decisions
- Health care advance directive

Creative and Constructive Planning

Help is available from friends, pastors, and professional advisors. Procrastination is your worst enemy. Procrastination places a heavy burden and weight on your soul!

Planning for the years in the second half of your life can be a most creative and constructive experience. Just like you plan where to go to college, which job to take, and where to move, you can plan your second half of life with diligence.

God wants you to be all that you can be. God loves you completely and you are called to finish your life well. Just because you are getting older and your identity is changing is no reason to discount the importance of living fully every day.

God loves you in unique ways. This love is what gives you wisdom, worth, and dignity. You then know how best to love others with caring conversations around your own mortality. Culture today tries to hide the reality of aging. And yet your faith teaches you how to live with physical limitations and unlimited wisdom. As one of God's people, your fears can fade and your faith can expand as God's spirit works to help you become more and more like Christ:

I say be guided by the Spirit and you won't carry out your selfish desires. A person's selfish desires are set against the Spirit, and the Spirit is set against one's selfish desires. They are opposed to each other, so you shouldn't do whatever you want to do. But if you are being led by the Spirit, you aren't under the Law. The actions that are produced by selfish motives are obvious, since they include sexual immorality, moral corruption, doing whatever

73

feels good, idolatry, drug use and casting spells, hate, fighting, obsession, losing your temper, competitive opposition, conflict, selfishness, group rivalry, jealousy, drunkenness, partying, and other things like that. I warn you as I have already warned you, that those who do these kinds of things won't inherit God's kingdom.

But the fruit of the Spirit is love, joy, peace, patience, kindness, goodness, faithfulness, gentleness, and self-control. There is no law against things like this. Those who belong to Christ Jesus have crucified the self with its passions and its desires.

If we live by the Spirit, let's follow the Spirit. Let's not become arrogant, make each other angry, or be jealous of each other. (Gal 5:16-26)

Spiritual Growth Opportunities

We can include personal growth opportunities in our planning. The older we get the more interest in personal and spiritual growth becomes apparent. There is a theology of aging that tells us that when we have had spiritual experiences with God in the past we anticipate eternal life and have limited fear of death.

Remember the story of Abraham and Sarah who were blessed to be a blessing because of their faithfulness and God's promises. Moses had a caring conversation with God about his call to free God's enslaved people. God would be with Moses, and Moses told God's people that they would know this through signs and power. Our God is not just a God of the past. God calls and equips the church and invites us to move forward to bring hope to the world. Hope is essential!

> *We have different gifts that are consistent with God's grace that has been given to us. If your gift is prophecy, you should prophesy in proportion to your faith. If you gift is service, devote yourself to serving. If your gift is teaching, devote yourself to teaching. If your gift is encouragement, devote yourself to encouraging. The one giving should do it with no strings attached. The leader should lead with passion. The one showing mercy should be cheerful.*
>
> *—Romans 12:6-8*

Learn from others who model a fulfilling second half of life. These people find ways to nurture their mind, heart, and soul. Take time to ask someone you respect about how he or she finds meaning in life.

Opportunities for Making an Impact

The second half of life also can bring opportunities for significant moral growth. You can have a significant impact on your community, church, and country if you stay involved.

Here are just a few ways you can bring justice and compassion to others:

- Be aware of how you treat others.
- Use your life experiences to serve others (mission).
- Discover stages of moral development.[2]
- Become an activist for the needs of others.

Significant spiritual growth is also vitally important for the second half of life. God empowers all intellectual, personal, moral, and spiritual growth. With God's help, you do not have to fall victim to fear, lack of control, and cynical thoughts and behavior.

Think about the things above and not things on earth.

—Colossians 3:2

Here are a few ways intentional spiritual growth can help you make the most of your life:

- By enhancing personal relationships with God and others
- By improving intellectual, personal, and moral development
- By spending time in prayer and Bible study
- By serving as spiritual guides and mentors
- By praying for others

- By teaching and instructing others
- By worshipping and celebrating God's blessings
- By assisting others to dicover the stages of spiritual growth
- By enhancing your comprehension of scripture and theological books

Assignment

Ask Yourself

- Is there anyone I need to have a caring conversation with about any of these topics?
- Is there any unfinished business I need to discuss?

Who you visit with will make a difference! Act this week!

Chapter 6
LEGACY PLANNING EMPOWERS LEGACY LIVING

Scripture Verse

The earth is the LORD's and everything in it, / the world and its inhabitants too.

—Psalm 24:1

Opening Prayer

Creator, Savior, and Redeemer, you give us everything we need for this life and the life to come. Show us how to respect the heritage of those who have come before us and to be responsible with the good gifts you have bestowed on us. Thank you. Amen.

Introduction

While some of the greatest challenges of retirement are emotional and relational, the financial challenges that many face are often unknown. Many don't have a spending plan and enter into the unknown with financial anxiety. We may not be able financially to retire so we will keep on working. We may even desire an "encore" job!

In any case, most people plan to live more modestly than before. People downsize and find ways to live with less money—but with more joy. Scripture says that fulfillment is not determined by finances alone. Contentment happens when you understand your financial situation clearly and live within your means. Yet, living within your means and leaving a legacy covers much more than just finances. Pastors who care for families at the time of the death of a loved one know that if the deceased had planned his or her legacy, family members experience healing of grief and greater joy and are able to celebrate a well-lived life that was filled with love, faith, hope, and charity.

Getting to Know You

If you have not retired, how long do you expect to work?

If you have retired from a career or have a spouse who has retired, how are you spending your time?

Will You Have a Purpose-Filled Second Half of Life?

John Wesley, the founder of the Methodist movement in the 1700s, lived and died as a generous man of God. He left a legacy of faith and love that informed and inspired the Methodist movement in England to give birth to a new church in America. As a result, Methodist Christians today know that good stewardship makes great generosity possible.

> *Make all you can, save all you can,*
> *and give all you can!*
>
> *—John Wesley*

Wesley knew that safeguarding one's legacy was an important consideration for all times of history. Over the years, you may have learned how to manage your money better. You may also have learned the painful consequences from financial failure. As people approach retirement, money management and good stewardship are essential to ensure a significant and successful road ahead.

In his sermon "Toward the Tithe and Beyond: How God Funds His Work," John Piper gives the example of John Wesley and his generosity.

> This so baffled the English Tax Commissioners that they investigated him in 1776 insisting that for a man of his income he must have silver dishes that he was not paying excise tax on. He wrote them, "I have two silver spoons at London and two at Bristol. This is all the plate I have at present, and I shall not buy any more while so many round me want bread."
>
> When he died in 1791 at the age of 87, the only money mentioned in his will was the coins to be found in his pockets and dresser.[1]

Wesley's example is a challenge as you seek to honor Christ with your money over your lifetime. It helps to remember, however, that it is all God's money anyway. Hold it with open hands.

Bill's Story

(As told by Dave Wilson)

Bill is a retired clinical scientist whose journey into retirement is just starting. He was blessed in a job environment that allowed him to travel the world researching new medicines. It was challenging and stimulating, but there was also great pressure to get things done. His last years in the business helped Bill develop a mentoring and teaching mentality to help others do their jobs better. When he talked to friends who had retired, he began to see how this skill could be part of his retirement future. With good financial planning for retirement, he was ready to make the change.

His initial view of retirement was a "Barcalounger": personal comfort, just enjoy life as much as he wanted, travel, do personal study, and take guitar lessons. But it didn't take long for Bill to see that there were activities that God wanted him to do and they didn't include sitting on the couch and dying. He needed to give something back for the betterment of the nonreligious and nominally religious people about whom his church is so concerned.

Among the aspects of retirement that Bill found exciting were that he would no longer have the daily grind and would have a flexible schedule to do things that mattered most. He would be able to try new things in his second half of life story that is just beginning to develop.

Several events helped Bill begin to have a significant retirement. First, his health stabilized and he is getting in shape for this new lifestyle. Second, he met a mentor who is helping him steer into new opportunities of service in his community.

Although he does not yet have a mission statement, he was always a goal setter in his professional life and planning his mission statement is a good way to maximize his ideas.

Bill has great passions in life, starting with Jesus Christ and his church. He also loves to travel the world as he did when was researching new medicines. Bill's profession allowed him to become a generous giver, allowing him to set up small business and personal loans to people in Africa. He is passionate about relationships and his University of Kentucky school ties. He is a Kentucky basketball fan, loves music, plays guitar, sings in the choir, sees many movies, and is active in the local Rotary Club. With his passion for world travel, medicine, and music he seems pointed in the direction of medical mission trips and music missions as part of a band.

Bill is part of the John Wesley Legacy Society of his church. This group of people in the Wesley Society has decided to leave a legacy gift to sustain the future ministry, mission, and facility needs of their church. This will make a difference for decades to come.

Questions for Discussion

1. What are the key elements of Bill's story?

_____

_____

_____

2. How do you relate to his story?

_____

_____

_____

3. What is the next step you will take?

_____

_____

_____

Understanding the Bible Story

Read 1 Timothy 6:6-11. How does Paul encourage and warn Timothy?

_____

_____

_____

What do you learn in the passage that you can apply to yourself?

_____

_____

_____

> *I'm already being poured out like a sacrifice to God, and the time of my death is near. I have fought the good fight, finished the race, and kept the faith.*
>
> *—2 Timothy 4:6-7*

Read Malachi 3:10. How does God challenge Malachi's readers in biblical times and you today regarding money?

_____

_____

_____

What is your plan for your money in retirement? Do you have a budget and an advisor you trust?

_____

_____

_____

Read Matthew 6:19-21. What does Jesus teach us here about legacies?

_____

_____

_____

Small Group Discussion Questions

Who are some of the people who left a legacy that influences you? (These can be famous, such as Mother Teresa, or a person known just to you, such as a grandparent.)

What are your thoughts about leaving a legacy of faithful witness, good works, and/or financial resources to your family, your church, and causes you value?

How do you want to be remembered? What do you need to do now to make that dream happen?

How can leaving a legacy for those you love and causes you value bring purpose and fulfillment to your retirement years?

Experiencing Your Life Story

For a legacy to make a difference, it needs to be communicated to others or written down to be read by others when you are deceased. You may not be ready to transition into heaven, but now is the time for you to plan how you will finish well. What would you like to pass on to your family? Have you taken time to journal the treasures of your heart? Can you write out your witness of faith and love for your family and friends? Can you prepare a list for your family to know which music, readings, and stories you want for your own funeral and celebration of life?

> *Our real legacy resides in the life we leave behind, the spiritual treasures we have stored in heaven.*
>
> —*Richard Morgan,* Pilgrimage into the Last Third of Life

Recording Important Information

As this study has emphasized, being prepared is the most important thing you can do to bless your family, friends, church, and charity. Too often families are burdened with too many loose ends, not enough information, and financial matters that are not recorded. They may not know where you keep your important records or if you have a list of passwords to your online accounts or the names and contact information of your attorney and financial advisor. What success have you had in accomplishing some of these tasks?

Document the following personal records to make sure your legacy is in order:

- Memorial/funeral planning (favorite music, scripture, memorial funds)
- Obituary and tribute
- Burial or cremation arrangements
- Insurance records
- Will or trust documents
- Property disbursement (homes, automobiles, household items, heirlooms, etc.)
- Updated financial statement (bank accounts, brokerage accounts, pension accounts, IRA accounts, other assets/liabilities)
- Computer program/website password list

This information and other family records need to be kept in at least two locations. Many people put this information is a safe place at home and also in their safe-deposit box at a bank. Ask your church if a personal affairs record keeper is available. If not, create your own. See Tool H: Legacy Planning for more information.

Legacy Planning

Living Your Legacy Planning Checklist

Check those areas that need discussion and planning.

Family/Friends Relationship

_____ Children

_____ Grandchildren

_____ New friends

_____ Longtime friends

Financial

_____ Investment/spending percentage planning ratios

_____ Annual budget/spending plan

_____ Available savings

_____ Investments

_____ Conservative/risk factors

_____ Cost of living

_____ Social Security

_____ Money sharks

_____ Donations to church and charity

_____ Estate planning

Health

_____ Preventive care

_____ Medical care

_____ Insurance costs

_____ Medications

_____ Reality diet

_____ Health directives

_____ Exercise options

Where to Live?

_____ Near family

_____ Near friends

_____ Retirement locations

_____ Retirement communities

_____ Multiple locations

Hobbies

_____ Personal

_____ Group

Travel

_____ Short/long trips

_____ Timeshares

_____ Tourist traps

Mentoring

_____ Professional

_____ Family

_____ Friends

Time Management

_____ Part-time work

_____ Volunteering

_____ Church service

_____ Community service

Faith

_____ Study

_____ Worship

_____ Service

_____ Mission

_____ Fellowship

_____ Generosity

_____ Spiritual growth

Legacy

_____ Percentage model/dollar amounts

_____ Completing your will or trust

_____ Family

_____ Church

_____ Charity

_____ Heirlooms

_____ Written funeral requests

_____ Journal or life history/highlights

_____ Words of thanks to family and friends

_____ Values/how do you want to be remembered?

Dying Well

_____ Guardianships

_____ Power of attorney

_____ Health directives

_____ Planning for your memorial service

_____ Leaving a written blessing for others

Lifelong Learning

_____ Classes at church

_____ Classes at university

_____ Mental growth

_____ Moral/ethical growth

Community Involvement

_____ Civic clubs

_____ Political causes

_____ Sports

Recommended Resources

Buford, Bob. *Beyond Halftime: Practical Wisdom for Your Second Half of Life*. Grand Rapids: Zondervan, 2008.

————. *Finishing Well: The Adventure of Life Beyond Halftime*. Grand Rapids: Zondervan, 2011.

————. *Game Plan: Winning Strategies for the Second Half of Your Life*. Grand Rapids: Zondervan, 1998.

————. *Halftime: Moving from Success to Significance*. Grand Rapids: Zondervan, 2008.

————. *Stuck in Halftime: Reinvesting Your One and Only Life*. Grand Rapids: Zondervan, 2001.

Cartmill, Carol, and Yvonne Gentile. *Serving from the Heart: Finding Your Gifts and Talents for Ministry*. Nashville: Abingdon Press, 2011.

Kohlberg, Lawrence. *The Philosophy of Moral Stages and the Idea of Justice: Essays on Moral Development*. Vol. 1. New York: Harper and Row, 1981.

Ministry Matters. www.ministrymatters.com.

Notes

Introduction

1. D'Vera Cohn and Paul Taylor, "Baby Boomers Approach 65—Glumly: Survey Findings about America's Largest Generation," *Pew Research Center*, December 20, 2010, http://www.pewsocialtrends.org/files/2010/12/Boomer-Summary-Report-FINAL.pdf.

1. Discovering Your Life Story

1. Diane Cole, "Why You Need to Find a Mission," *The Wall Street Journal*, January 13, 2013, http://www.wsj.com/articles/SB10001424127887323316804578163501792318298.

2. Transitions

1. Carol Cartmill and Yvonne Gentile, *Serving from the Heart: Finding Your Gifts and Talents for Service*, rev. ed. (Nashville: Abingdon Press, 2011).

4. Joy for the Journey

1. Ken Robinson, *The Element: How Finding Your Passion Changes Everything* (New York: Penguin Group, 2009).

5. Caring Conversations with Family and Friends

1. Iyanla Vanzant, 2004, http://www.iyanla.com/.

2. Jane Marie Thibault and Richard Morgan, *Pilgrimage into the Last Third of Life: 7 Gateways to Spiritual Growth* (Nashville: The Upper Room, 2012).

6. Legacy Planning Empowers Legacy Living

1. John Piper, "Toward the Tithe and Beyond: How God Funds His Work" (sermon, Bethlehem Baptist Church, September 10, 1995), http://www.soundofgrace.com/piper95/09-10-95.htm.

Visit Cokesbury.com to download a free leader's guide PDF. Password: Cvqq8Nm

CPSIA information can be obtained
at www.ICGtesting.com
Printed in the USA
LVOW04s0245040616

491175LV00001B/1/P